Cartooning for Kids

Cartooning for Kids

Carol Lea Benjamin

A Harper Trophy Book

Harper & Row, Publishers

For my mother, Helen Kahn Hein,
who always made me eat what was good
for me so that I could grow up
to be a cartoonist.

Library of Congress Cataloging in Publication Data
Benjamin, Carol.
Cartooning for kids.
Summary: Outlines how to draw simple cartoons from circles,
dots, lines, and curves and how to add professional
touches such as shading, decorative detail, or color.
1. Cartooning—Juvenile literature.   [1. Cartooning.
2. Drawing—Technique]   I. Title.
NC1320.B38 1982   741.5   81-43876
ISBN 0-690-04207-8   AACR2
ISBN 0-690-04208-6 (lib. bdg.)
ISBN 0-06-446063-0 (pbk.)

Contents

So What If You Can't Draw!   1

Sad, Mad, Bad, Glad   13

Body Basics   24

Everything Else You Have to Know
About Drawing   29

What's So Funny?   33

Some Surprising Sources   44

Still Funny After All These Years   52

Funny, Funnier, Funniest   57

Professional Secrets You Can Use   62

Spin-Offs   68

A Glossary of Animal Characters

So What
If You Can't Draw!

No one really knows who drew the first cartoon or even when it was drawn. Perhaps one day long ago a cave man wanted to warn his tribe that a hungry pterodactyl was in the neighborhood. He'd never drawn a picture in his life. Then again, there was no written language yet, so he couldn't leave a note.

He found a sharp rock. He saw a blank wall, halfway between a stalagmite and a picture of a Tyrannosaurus rex. Then he changed history: he drew the first cartoon. His drawing had a dual effect: it carried a powerful mes-

1

sage, and it made someone laugh. It might have looked something like this:

You don't need a cave or a pointy rock to become a cartoonist. All you need is an ordinary pencil and some unlined paper. You don't have to be an artist. In fact, you don't need any special talents. If you can draw a circle, you're in business.

This book will show you how to cartoon. It will help you to find out how to reduce the elaborate, complicated-looking creatures and objects you see around you to easy-to-draw circles, dots, lines, and curves. It will show you how to make simple drawings look professional by adding shading, decorative details, or color. It will help you to find the hidden humor in ordinary and extraordinary situations. It will even show you how to use your cartoons to make greeting cards, business cards, and notes that will definitely be read. As you will soon discover, cartooning can be both enjoyable and easy.

Get some paper and a pencil. You're going to begin by drawing a circle. Don't worry if the circle isn't perfectly round or if the beginning and the end of the circle don't meet. It doesn't matter. Don't jump ahead and try to copy the finished character. Even if the steps look easy to you, you're more likely to draw the character well if you go step by step.

Cartoon Animals

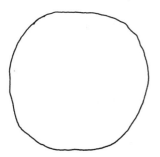

1. Draw a circle.

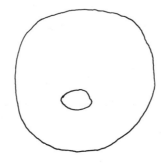

2. Draw a smaller oval in the lower half of the circle.

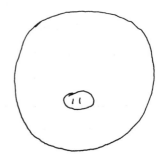

3. Two little vertical lines in the oval become nostrils. Dots would work just as well.

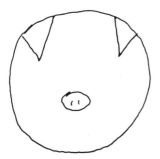

4. Draw two small triangles for ears.

5. Two small vertical lines become eyes. Now your drawing will look like this.

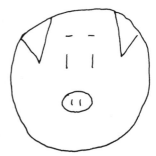

6. Short horizontal lines look like eyebrows.

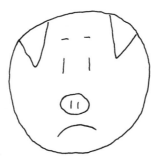 

7. This character needs a mouth. It's just a small curve.

8. Hey! That's upside down.

9. Ah. Good work, cartoonist! Give your pig a name and . . .

10. some lunch.

Now you can begin to go faster because the following characters have many of the same features as the first.

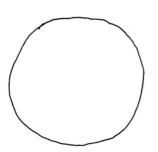

1. Draw a circle.

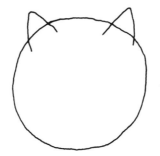

2. Add standing ears. Don't worry about the overlapping lines. You are working in pencil so you can erase them at the end.

3. You probably already know what animal this is. Give it eyes and eyebrows.

4. Use a small triangle for the nose.

5. Make the mouth by drawing two j's, back to back. Add whiskers.

6. Add a fish.

1. Draw a circle, but place it lower on the page to leave room for . . .

2. big, standing ears.

3. I thought I said "big, *standing* ears."

4. Draw eyes and eyebrows. Draw a tiny circle for a nose and two back-to-back j's for a mouth.

5. Good rabbit!

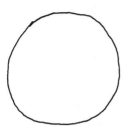  

1. Draw a circle.

2. Draw eyes and eye-brows and a mouth.

3. Draw round, standing ears and you've got . . . a bear!

Cartoon People

Some cartoonists draw animals that speak and act as if they were human. Others draw human characters. You'll find that cartoon people are as easy to draw as cartoon animals. Here are a few.

1. Draw a circle. Draw eyes and eyebrows.

2. Draw a mouth. The nose can be a smaller version of a smiling mouth, turned upside down.

3. Add messy hair . . .

4. or neat hair . . .   **5.** or curly hair . . .   **6.** or girly hair.

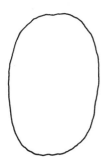

And what's a kid . . .   without . . .   a pal?

Cartooning Means Shortcuts

Cartoons are drawings that get the most mileage possible from the least amount of detail:

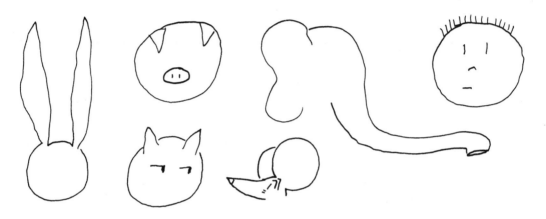

When you see something you'd like to draw, first try to reduce it to the fewest possible lines. Omit as many details as you can. This will help you to develop a knack for taking artistic shortcuts.

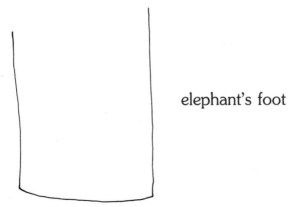

elephant's foot

Cartooning Means Details

Once you have a simplified drawing, take a second look at it. Try to discover what there is about this particular person, animal, or object that is not only essential, but especially wonderful, magical, and characteristic of the something you were going to draw. Those are the details you will want to use. They will make your drawing not merely recognizable, but interesting and "characterful."

For example, you would never want to leave out . . .

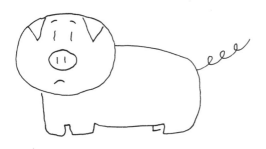

a pig's tail . . .

dad's moustache . . .

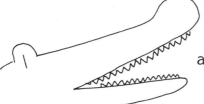

an alligator's teeth . . .

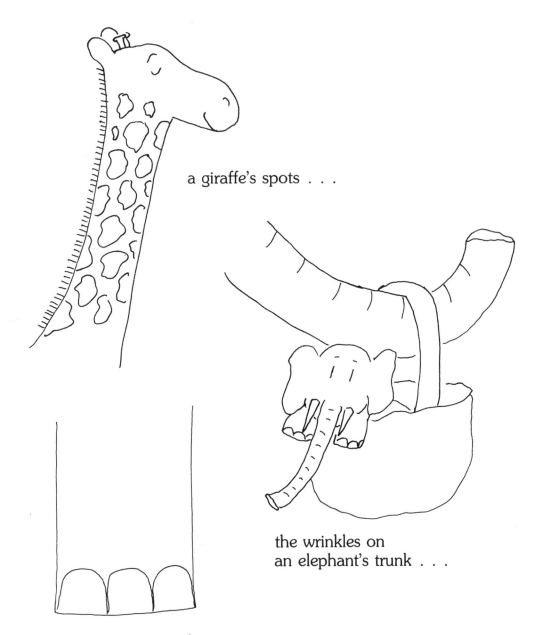

a giraffe's spots . . .

the wrinkles on
an elephant's trunk . . .

or its gigantic toenails.

Sad, Mad,
Bad, Glad

In some cartoons the humor does not depend on the expressions on a character's face.

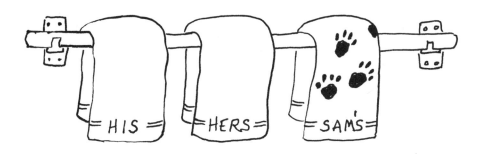

In other cartoons the emotional reaction is all!

In cartooning you need to know how to make your characters laugh, cry, look surprised, look smart or stupid, get angry, or look smug, nervous, or happy. That may sound like a tall order, but it isn't. You can represent most of these feelings with just a slight shift in the slant of an eyebrow, for example, or the curve of the mouth.

Here is one of the basic faces from the first chapter. Watch what happens to the eyes, the eyebrows, and the mouth.

BASIC
FACE

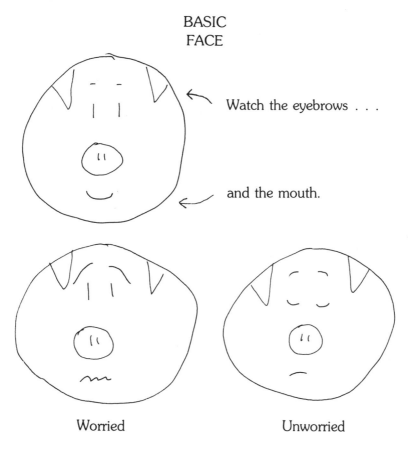

Watch the eyebrows . . .

and the mouth.

Worried   Unworried

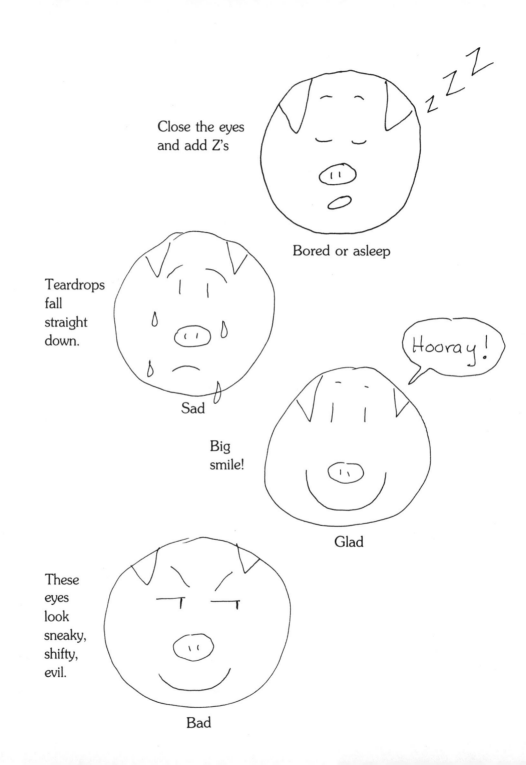

Sweat shoots out to the side. It and the changes in the eyes, eyebrows, and mouth make the character look very scared.

Scared

Mad

Smug

Knowing how to convey emotions allows you to turn a very simple idea into a cartoon. Here, one character speaks and another reacts. Just the right reaction will make you and your friends laugh.

Or your characters can emote when they're all alone. Here is a situation with five possible endings. Each solution is based on a different emotional reaction to the problem at hand. Try a similar series with one of the other characters and then decide which ending you find funniest. By experimenting in this fashion you will see how useful it is to be able to have your characters make faces.

Here's the problem . . .

and here's how it looks with each of five different solutions.

Now you have the freedom to show emotion or not. You will be able to give your character a deadpan look when that's appropriate . . .

or convey any deep emotion that suits your imagination and your joke.

Now you can make your characters look mad,

sad,   bad,

and glad!

Body Basics

A cartoon character can manage very well with a simple, easy-to-draw body. You can differentiate between a pig, a cat, a rabbit, a bear, a dog, and a person by making small changes in the hands and feet, or by adding a tail. If you are going to make your cartoon animals talk, you may want to draw them upright, as if they were two-legged creatures.

Once you know how to draw the basic face and body, you can begin to experiment with individual details. Draw a page of noses, a page of feet, a page of hands and paws. Hands can be difficult to draw, but you have two built-in models with you all the time! By practicing details, you will gradually improve your basic characters, enriching them with huge noses, expressive hands, toes coming through the ends of shoes, and even funny hats and outfits. But there's no rush about adding these special touches. If you can draw expressive faces and basic bodies, you can do complete and interesting cartoons.

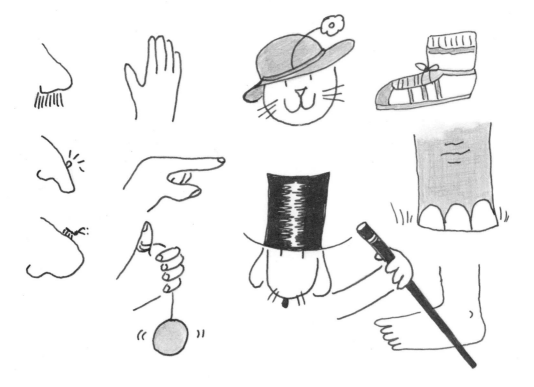

Things to Do

1. Trace your favorite cartoon characters from comic books and magazines. Then draw them with changes: different hair, a funnier nose, bigger feet.

2. Try drawing one of your own characters in several different positions: standing, sitting, lying in bed, running, eating, talking on the phone, slipping on a banana peel, laughing.

Everything Else You Have to Know About Drawing

Suppose you have a cartoon in mind that requires a haunted house or a supersonic transport or a beagle puppy. Would you remember enough of what each one looks like to make your drawing of it recognizable? Probably not. You might think you do, but when you actually try to draw the dog, you may find that it looks more like a spaniel than a beagle. As a cartoonist, you will want and need the freedom to draw anything and everything that strikes you as funny. You won't want to be limited to drawing cartoons about the few things you can draw from memory. Good news! You don't have to be. You can keep a picture file, just as most professional cartoonists do.

A picture file is a collection of pictures from magazines and newspapers, filed in alphabetical order according to subject. Whenever you get a chance, add to your picture file and keep it growing. Then when you want to put a car, an elephant, a castle, or a Spanish dancer into one of your cartoons, you can take a picture of it from the file to see what it looks like. If something you need isn't in your file yet, don't give up. Use pictures in an encyclopedia or a book, or draw from real life. Always make it a habit to look at the real thing before you draw. It will make your drawings much better and much more interesting. Once cartooned, the object will be less realistic, less detailed, freer, and funnier, but it won't be less accurate. You won't put pointed ears on a chimp or sails on a submarine. People will see what you intend them to see, and inaccuracy will not stand in the way of your good jokes.

Photographs are among the richest picture sources you will ever find because the pictures can be so personal. Photographs will do more than help you to draw things so that they are recognizable—they will allow you to make cartoon characters of friends and family without asking them to sit and pose for long hours. A good snapshot can even help you turn yourself into a cartoon character! Notice how the drawings change the photographs yet keep the flavor of the original.

All photographs by Noah A. Kahn.

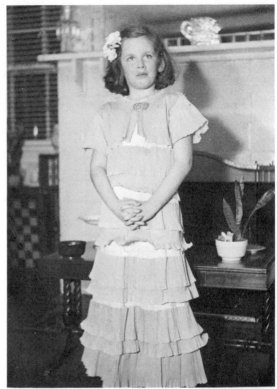

What's So Funny?

Now you have a small family of characters who can express a useful range of emotions. Does this mean that you are ready to sit down and draw funny cartoons? Yes! Sometimes funny ideas will come easily, as if they had flown in through the window. You'll get a flash and be able to put it on paper. But there will be other times when you will feel like cartooning and funny ideas won't come. If you sit down and try to be funny, you may go blank. Don't worry. That's when you must go hunting. Armed with only a pencil, a pad, and a fierce, attack-

33

trained brain, you must venture into the wilds of your own mind and poke around for gags.

One way to be a successful hunter is to know *what* you're after. In other words, you must first choose your prey. Narrow your focus from the whole wide world to a single, specific subject. Zero in on *anything* that tickles *you*. It doesn't matter what subject you choose, as long as you find it funny.

How to Brainstorm

Once you've made a selection, the next step is to brain-storm for possible jokes about that topic. Begin by asking yourself all kinds of questions about your subject, questions based on your own normal, everyday activities. Something special about your subject may well result in answers to the questions that will inspire funny cartoons. Here's an example of how to go about it.

SNAKES

1. *How would a snake eat, or play with its friends?*

2. *Do snakes worry about how they look, what they are getting for their birthdays, or what's for dinner? What do snakes worry about?*

3. Since a snake has no legs how would it get around? How would it ride a bike or use roller skates? How would it ride in a car or on a bus?

4. What would a snake learn in school? What could it do that was good or bad?

5. Would a snake sleep in a bed? Would it sleep over or under the covers? Would it use a teddy bear?

Experiment. Sketch as many cartoons as you can think of on one or two or three or more worksheets. The cartoons won't all be funny. Who cares? No one will see your work unless you decide to show it.

If you get stuck on one topic, choose another one. If you go blank in the middle of a cartoon, put it aside and go on. You may find a way to make it hilarious another day.

Be nice and loose when you are trying to be funny. Don't try to bully cartoons out. Coax out the jokes.

Here are some more examples of how your hunt will work.

ANIMALS ACTING HUMAN

CAVE PEOPLE

LOVE

Things to Do

1. *See how many funny cartoons you can draw by brainstorming about the following topics:*

allowance	talking computers	flying saucers
school	homework	elephants
being good	being bad	monsters
pollution	the circus	elves

2. *Begin to keep a list of funny topics. Keep the list handy so that you can add to it whenever something strikes you as funny.*

Some
Surprising Sources

Here's another good method for hunting down funny cartoons. Instead of using topics as your sources, use your favorite old stories or rhymes: myths and legends, Bible stories, famous tales about kings or presidents, Mother Goose rhymes, fairy tales. Try adding a modern element to an old tale, a bit of twentieth-century technology, for instance.

Here are some examples of what replacing something old with something new can do for the story of Cinderella . . .

and "The Three Little Pigs."

Or try giving a character the benefit of an outspoken, independent, up-to-date personality:

A change as minor as an updated hairstyle can result
in a funny cartoon.

Or you can try setting nursery rhymes in the twentieth century. Here, too, you will find ready-made stories just waiting for your comic twist.

Even serious subjects, such as religion, have their lighter sides. Poking gentle fun at something need not show disrespect; it can show knowledge and affection. Think of

how funny modern concerns or modern thinking would
have been in the Garden of Eden . . . or just before the
Flood.

Things to Do

1. *Use color! Color your cartoons with crayons, colored pencils, or watercolor paints. Often a little color is better than a lot. Try color in one main element that you want your audience to notice. Use color for emphasis and beauty.*

2. *Cover a bulletin board in your room with cartoons— your own or other people's! Doing this will help new ideas to pop into your head. It will get you lots of compliments. It will keep you thinking CARTOON!*

51

Still Funny After All These Years

There are two more sources for cartoons that every cartoonist should investigate: stock lines and stock situations. Some of these classics have been around forever. But if you think that means they are worn-out, just watch the magazines. Cartoonists are always looking with a fresh eye at classic lines and situations, turning out funny, brand-new cartoons. You can do it, too.

Here are some wonderful stock lines accompanied by new cartoons. Fool around with these yourself. You may find you can go on and on, doing three, four, or five different drawings to illustrate one old, but not tired, line.

Here are some more classic lines, just waiting for you to breathe new life into them.

1. *Gee, can't I keep him? He followed me home.*
2. *What did I do now?*
3. *Are you sure this is the right road?*
4. *Make believe you don't see him.*
5. *I don't know what we would have done without him.*
6. *Either he goes, or I go!*
7. *I've just washed my hair and I can't do a thing with it.*
8. *You'll never guess what I did today.*

You can work with stock situations, too. Here are a few, still funny after all these years.

The desert island . . .

YOU ARE HERE

A sign can make the most ordinary scene funny. That's why one of the great stock situations is a scene with a sign.

Ever since the Great Depression when formerly wealthy businessmen went out on the street to sell apples, the idea of someone selling matches, pencils, or apples on the street has been a classic situation for cartoonists. Sooner or later, every cartoonist seems to want to give it a try.

And here are a few more. See how many of them inspire you to do new twists on old favorites.

1. *Someone slipping on a banana peel.*
2. *A princess kissing a frog.*
3. *A sign that says "Last chance for gas."*
4. *A thirsty man crawling in the desert.*
5. *Someone on a scale reading a fortune card.*
6. *Someone asking Santa for Christmas presents.*
7. *Robots or computers acting human.*

Funny, Funnier, Funniest

When you first begin to draw cartoons, you will be overjoyed when you get a funny idea—as well you should be. After a while, though, you may want to make some of those funny flashes even funnier. There is a way to punch up your jokes and get richer, louder, longer laughs.

Here's the magic formula: stick with it! Instead of jumping around from joke to joke, stay with one idea or line. Work it over and over again until you can say, "Now *that's* funny!"

Here's an example using a visual image. Suppose it struck you that cowboy clothes look pretty funny, unless they're on a cowboy. Ask yourself when they would look the funniest. Suppose a baby wore them? What would happen if *everyone* wore them?

Keep going. (After all, you may like the whole page of cartoons, from first to last.) How about a grandmother in cowboy clothes? Or do you have a pet? Try drawing it in cowboy duds. Keep experimenting, and see where it all goes.

You can work in the same way with a single line. It can be a line you hear all the time—one from TV, for instance—or a line you make up yourself. Draw the first cartoon that comes to mind to illustrate the funny line. But don't stop there. Stick with your line and keep making changes in the illustrations.

59

The message in this chapter is simple, but important. Don't stop at your first idea. Keep working on it: exaggerate it, understate it, switch the characters around, add animals, try new captions. Keep messing with the idea until it brings the biggest laugh possible. Then do your finished piece and show it around.

Professional Secrets You Can Use

Y̲ou can draw hilarious cartoons with a plain pencil. Fancy and expensive equipment won't make your jokes any funnier! However, switching from a pencil to an inexpensive marking pen will give your cartoons a sharper, more finished look.

Here's Spot plain, drawn with

an ordinary #2 pencil,

an inexpensive marking pen,

an expensive mechanical drawing pen.

A pencil is easy to use and inexpensive. It allows you to erase and thus improve your work.

Markers come in many widths, from very thin to very thick. They are readily available and most cost less than one dollar. It's a good idea always to work in pencil first. Then when you are satisfied with your pencil drawing, trace over the lines with a marker.

Mechanical pens are very expensive, need frequent cleaning in order to work properly and get ruined in no time if neglected. Wait until you sell your first cartoon before you buy one.

Techniques used by professional cartoonists won't make your jokes any funnier, but they will

1. *draw attention to a part of your cartoon to help people see what's funny,*
2. *make your cartoons more interesting,*
3. *make your cartoons more attractive,*
4. *give your cartoons variety, and*
5. *provide you with new skills that are fun to use.*

Here's Spot fancy

with spots,   with shading,   with wash.

Outline the spots first and then fill them in with pencil or pen. Use the side of your pencil to shade a drawing.

Wash can only be used on good-quality drawing paper. Put a drop of black ink or watercolor in a little dish of water and paint it on with a small brush.

Backgrounds are beautiful! You can add even more life and interest to your cartoons by adding weather.

Use simple outlines for the
sun or moon, or for
clouds, flowers, and trees.

Small vertical lines give
the impression of rain.
You don't need drops.

Now when you see shadows, patterns, or spots in published cartoons, you will understand how they were made. You will be able to analyze the technique and recreate it in your own cartoons. Soon you will be inventing designs and patterns of your own, adding wallpaper, fabric, falling leaves, and lightning to your cartoons, too.

To make snow, paint the area with black ink. When it is thoroughly dry, dab on thick, white poster paint with the tip of your brush.

Spin-offs

Knowing how to draw appealing cartoon characters and how to create amusing situations can have some fringe benefits. You can use your new skills to make greeting cards and business cards or to illustrate the notes you write. Here's how.

Making Your Own Greeting Cards

Once you know how to draw cartoons, making greeting cards becomes a snap. Use plain white paper. Fold a piece in half and then in half again. Now you have a blank card that you can turn into a birthday, holiday, or gift card.

Cover

Inside

Making Business Cards

Have you always wanted to say, "My card!"? Now you can.

Use any heavy white paper. Sometimes white cardboard comes in new shirts, so it's free. Or buy a large sheet of two-ply bristol board at an art supply store. Cut your paper to standard business-card size, 3½" by 2".

Since you will do each card by hand, each can be different—an individual work of art. Business cards are fun to use, and they make terrific gifts. You can even make one for your dog!

Writing the World's Most Attention-Getting Notes

Do you hate to be ignored? Do you sometimes feel that no one pays attention to the important things you have to say? Friend, begin to leave illustrated notes. *Nobody* can resist a note with a cartoon on it. You'll have a good time. You'll save wear and tear on your voice box. You'll get your message across.

71

A Glossary of Animal Characters

Here are some other characters you can use in your cartoons. Each was drawn from a photograph from my picture file. Each is easier to draw than it looks. If you like, you can trace the characters first. Then try them freehand, ignoring the details—the spots, fur, and so on. Once your outline drawing is completed, corrected, and inked, then you can add the frills.

Bat

Mother and child . . . and banana

Goose and mouse

If you can make bricks, you can make a turtle.

whale

Important note: Draw what you see. Then draw what you wish you could see—an anteater being outsmarted by an ant, a penguin in a top hat, a talking giraffe.

Anteater

Owl

Cute giraffe

Penguin acting silly